Musings on the Life of the Soul

Robert Malouf

Contents

1. Along the Path

Along the Path,

A Maiden fair
With verses to awaken
Ages yet unborn
And generations consigned
To sepulchers of neglect,
Shows me signs
And tokens
Of Impenetrable Mystery –
I bear witness
To irrefutable Truths
That flow from her lips
Into the streams and brooks
Of my soul.

Confusion

Flees from my being,
Veils,
Anchors of blindness,
Descend the depths
Of the stale,
Murky waters
Of blind imitation
To rise no more.

We walk,

Hand in hand –
Ascend the path
To Paradise.
Words and letters
Stir the heart.
Principles all-glorious,
Law too beauteous
And fair
To bear description,
Line our way.
Their blossoms,
Extravagant in number,
Scent the air
With jasmine, honeysuckle,
Hyacinth,
Lilac and rose –
Fragrances telling tales
Of love's possibilities.
These penetrate the core
Of my soul.

What path is this,

I walk?
What Maiden so fair
That I am captive to,
Enthralled by,
Her Beauty?
My heart,
Captured
By her exquisite, inviolable
Profundity –
Ineffable
Beyond all description
And rushing forth from lips
Ruby red
That shine like the sun
And allure as if moonglow,
These but a token
Of Her Beauty –
Need not ask!

At last,

With eyes anew
And heart on fire
As if a volcano were welling up,
Surging within me,
I say –
"O, Celestial Damsel!
Beauteous Maiden
Bearing
Gifts of Truth!
What name have you,
You who are adorned
As a Bride
Descending from Heaven
On the Promised
Day of God?"

Piercing my soul,

Searching
For purity and longing within me
To grasp it,
She intones
At Heaven's Door,
"I am the Word of God,
Begotten
By the Pen of Glory.
Come!
Walk with me.
Our journey,
Short or long,
Has only begun."

"Behold!

I am your fast,
True Companion
Whose Countenance,
Born of Glory,
Illumines your way.
I am
The All-Beauteous Guide
To the All-Glorious,
He Who seeks with Holy Love
Eternal,
Hearts illumined
From the lamps of detachment,
Souls shining
In resplendent hues of prized humility –
These,
True lovers
In search
Of the Beloved."

2. As One

As one,

They danced
Atop the page
Two by two,
Rhythm
And rhyme,
Sound
And syllable,
In God-like
Choreography.

First,

They rose to heaven
In angelic grace,
Danced
Whisper soft
Upon wind and cloud,
Then circled the moon,
Eclipsing
Its splendor.

I saw them dive

To ocean deeps
Heretofore unknown –
Electrify ocean floor
To life.

Not restrained

To such awesome display,
They raced and tumbled
In acrobat-like precision,
Synchronized,
Upon fast-rushing,
Billowing waves,
Dove,
In true abandon,
Deep
Into their swallowing troughs,
Only to rise,
Feather-like,
To frolic upon
Light-hearted
Sprays.

As one,

They danced
Atop the page
And rode the high winds
Of meaning,
Traversed mountains
Of knowledge,
And dove the deep falls
Of profundity
And understanding.

I saw them God-like,

More heavenly
Than the Pleiades –
As, indeed,
They were,
And ever,
Will be.

3. Autumn Leaves

*In honor of those whose lives, on the pathway of Truth, were
taken from them.*

Autumn leaves fall

In measured gusts to eager ground
To be held dear in close
Embrace.

Once green, vibrant,

Photosynthetic,
Now clothed in quiet colors
Of red, amber and gold,
They fly high in strong winds,
Then low,
To rest, at last,
On the canopy
Where life is born and nourished
With each spring.

With each leaf

Memories are recalled
Of lives lived
And lost,
Of laughter,
Births,
And warm joys
Too dear to drop from recollection.

I am remembering the Beloved's

Lovers
Who, like the leaves,
Have journeyed to their last abode
To be embraced and held dear
By a small expanse of ground.

In their fall

They shone splendrous
In glorious hues
Of red, amber
And gold,
Untainted,
Undefiled,
By the tyrannical, howling winds
Loosed against them.

4. Bay Window

Musings on a Wisconsin winter day

Bay window,

Friend to my soul,
Through you
I see creation,
Exquisite maiden
That she is,
Her natural beauty
Sublime.
Her breathing –
Through flourishes
And halts
Of purifying winds –
Stands as testimony
To her impenetrable
Mystery.

Zephyrs,

Like bows on a string,
Caress her branches,
Giving rise to melodies
That whisper love songs
And tales past and future.
Her moonglow illumines
A cryptic glimpse into
Wonderment.
Her supernal skies,
Born by pillars of hope,
Beg contemplation.

Breathless beauty and wisdom

Are hers.
These challenge mind
And heart.
From her,
Life bursts forth
And enigma yields
To meaning.
From her bosom
Hymns of praise
And purpose
Rise and fly
In the face of gravity.
From her lips
Paeans of gratitude
Rejoice land and sea.

Her gaze

Awakens the soul,
Begets reflection.
Her stare
Opens to seeing eyes
Tokens –
Endless, diverse –
Of a Grand Creative Scheme
Of Purpose and Love.
It is for this,
She was created,
It is for this,
She dwells amongst us.

5. Beauty and Pain

*A long look at a portrait of a Native American elder many years
ago in San Francisco*

Through the glass

A long stare
At nobility
Tested by time
And struggle,
Proclaiming
The presence
Of beauty and pain,
Etched side by side,
Carved
By racing rivers
Of time,
Challenge,
Tribulation
And joy.

On that face,

Beauty,
Undeniably strong,
And pain,
Long-endured,
Deftly portrayed
By the artist's hand.

These,

Beauty and pain,
Will the Life Giver
And Begetter of every beauty
Resolve
On the Luminous Canvas
Of His Revelation,
A Canvas sweeping
From here to eternity,
Outstretched before all humanity,
And in heretofore unseen
Palettes
Of Ethereal Luminosity
And Truth
That, alone, dare paint,
At His Command
And by the brush strokes
Of His Mighty Pen,
Such a resolution.

6. Behind Closed Walls

Behind closed,

Stone walls
Black as coal,
Dense as diamond,
Mined from quarries
Of hardened human heart,
They eke out
Their shackled existence.

Pitch black cells

Cloaked in ignorance
Are their primary abode.
Windows to life,
Nailed
With empty thought
And closed by hands
Of empty dreams
Shut out hope,
Beauty,
Teleology.
From intellectual graveyards
They build their floors,
With blindness
They cover their dank,
Crumbling walls.
This they call
Living.

Offspring of materialism,

Stenchful,
Devouring,
Seemingly bacterial
In their omnipresence,
Rise and swarm
As flies of sin –
These they gather
And clutch close
To their bosom.
Birds of happiness
They call them.

Behind closed walls

In cells of darkness,
Beauty's Beloved
Is denied –
And Light's
Cheerful rays.
Playful,
Winsome breezes
Crash,
Retreat
Against impervious stone.
The air is hushed,
Foul,
Gasping
For renewal.
Energetic,
Promising dawns
Go unseen by sullen,
Downcast eyes.
Red and gold and brilliant
Transcend the vocabulary
Of this stygian place.
This they call
Seeing.

Hearts dark,

Occluded,
Thoughts low,
Coarse and hard,
These they drag about
Yet claim freedom
From imaginings'
Chain and ball.

Behind closed,

Stone walls,
In cells
Black as pitch,
Where the heart
Is pained
And the soul
Parched,
Where hope is lost
And torment reigns –
This is where the Beloved
Enters
With lamp in hand
To light the way.

7. Beside a Still Pond

Beside a still pond

I gazed into its quiet depths,
And saw but earthly dust
Against the reflections
Of a blue and white-clouded sky.
No trace of face or form
Did I see,
Only the few grains of inconsequence
That presented themselves.

My gaze turned to the mountains

Which stood as symbols
To the magnitude of my sins –
Wrongs of omission and commission
That would fill seemingly endless
Visible hillsides.

I looked upon the sky.

It is endless, lofty, majestic, magnificent.
I was reminded of my utter lowliness.
I stand, feet in place,
A gnat watching
A myriad soaring eagles.

Breezes blow

And acquaint me with their mysteries.
I listen but have no such tales to tell.
Bored,
They move on to other climes
Where souls are great and their stories long.

I behold the nighttime heavens

And am humbled by the stars.
They glisten brightly,
They burn endlessly
In their love for their Beloved –
The Beloved.

All created things whisper His Name,

Sing His praises,
Vibrate to His Beauty.
O, Lord in heaven,
Creator of all that has been
And will be,
Dispenser of endless,
Gleaming mercy,
Please tell me –
If they can,
Why can't I?

8. Black and White

Black and white

Upon the game board
Stare
In fixed,
Icy silence,
Each opposed,
Relentless,
Without mercy
Or care
For the other.

Hands,

Black and white,
Caring,
Bearing tests
Of time,
Moved by souls
Beating red,
Pulsating love,
Move carved, cold,
Lifeless pieces –
These bear no semblance,
Share no relationship,
To loving fingers,
Dark and light,
That move them.

Bodies,

Black and white,
Essences,
Translucent,
God's creation,
Uniquely beautiful,
Richly endowed,
Engage
In thoughtful,
Strategic play,
Their lives as one,
Freed
From icy stare,
Alive
To color,
Living gift
Born of time and place,
Breathtaking
In its
Diversity.

Souls,

Illumined,
Like shining eyes –
White,
Supportive,
At one
With pupils,
Black,
Light filled,
Each in need
Of the other –
Gaze
Heart to heart,
Radiant
In Love's Light,
Each
Fully alive
To the transcendent,
Multicolored
Magnificence
And beauty
Of the human
Flower garden.

9. Daffodils

Daffodils

Shine bright,
Soft,
Illumined yellow
Signs
Of early spring,
Testament
To gifts
Of earth and sky.
Their countenances,
Bright, golden,
Gladden
Heart and soul
And eye,
Extol unabashedly
The ineffable sweep
Of nature's beauty.

Wistful maidens,

Ashine in green and yellow,
Recite poetic verse
Born of beauty,
Edifying,
In light-filled whispers –
"In the soil of the heart
Plant love and tolerance,
That kindly windflowers
Spring forth,
Grow,
Be offered as bouquets
Of affection
And goodness."

Daffodils,

Wrapped in nature's
Adornment,
Rapturous
In their praise
Of the Eternal,
Proffer wisdom worthy
Of reflection –
"Let your words,
Softly flowing breezes,
Salubrious,
Refresh
Soul and heart –
Human flowers all-too-easily,
Like the daffodil,
Wilt
In harsh climes."

Luminous maids of delight,

Delicate beauties
Of Eternal Grace,
Wishful, wise, proclaim –
"Among tulips,
Dark and light –
Aside hyacinth
Redolent and vibrant –
Amidst roses red
And violets of every hue –
We dwell as one,
Our garden,
Beauteous,
Illumined
By the
One
Orb of life."

Golden maidens,

Atop emerald thrones,
In splendor
And profundity,
Speak to Truth –
"You, not we,
Are the true
And heavenly flowers,
Exquisitely diverse,
Arrayed in flawless color
From the brush strokes
Of the Heavenly Gardener –
Each to be honored
And loved –
Destined,
Like the infinite floral maidens
Painted from nature's palette,
To live and thrive,
In the Garden of His Love,
As one –
The birthright
Of every
Human flower.

10. Effulgent Beauty

Effulgent Beauty,

Light dancers circle about you,
Enthralled by dazzling luminosity
Penetrating the realities
Of all beings –
Their humility before the Throne of Glory
As a lowly mirror
Before the sun.

Splendorous Beauty,

No eye dare gaze into yours,
For, – and it must be so –
They would expire from fiery flames
Of penetrating love
That search, reveal, one's very worth –
This no creature can bear!

And should one chance a look upon

Your Resplendent Countenance,
The warming heat of your compassion
Might well enflame heart and mind with desire
To ride the restless zephyrs of longing
To the scarlet fields and blood-stained plains
Of sacrifice,
The true abode of mystic lovers
On fire, consumed,
With the blazing love
Of Your Glory.

O, Fiery Orb of Beauty!

No words have I to praise Godly Splendor,
For the pen retreats
And the ink languishes on the page,
Dark and cold.
Yet they call,
In utter feebleness,
"O Shining Globe of Manifestation,
May your Light be seen by all!
For the dark shroud of night
Has been too long,
And earthly response
To the Rising Dawn,
Remorsefully slow,
Long overdue.

11. Ethereal Beauty

Ethereal Beauty, windswept,

Soaring on heaven's winds,
Flying high above earthly pursuits,
Inspirer of all hearts,
Protector of souls,
Manifestation of the Unknowable –
Flap your wings Ethereal Beauty,
Fan the flame from which,
Reborn,
Phoenix-like,
Humanity must arise.
Shelter it beneath
Your shadow.

Should it falter,

Lift it up
To a higher vision,
A loftier nest
Closer to the heavens
In which you soar.

Sweep down

Majestic Bird of Heaven,
Grasp within your talons
All evil from us.
Free us
Of our lowly,
Three-dimensional stare,
Raise our necks
To follow your heavenly ascent
To where the future flies
And the present longs for,
Newly winged,
Faltering,
Determined.

Ethereal Beauty,

Prized Falcon
Of the All-Conquering King,
All dominion
Is yours to claim.
Rise high,
Sweep low,
Make us long to fly
Where past generations
Dared not go.

12. Fleeting Shadows

Fleeting shadows,

Passers by,
Frolicking pretenders
Masquerading as life,
Dark foam on waves of fancy –
You are but lifeless reminders
Of the Light that is,
Failed actors
On the coal-black stage
Of the benighted heart.
Yet, you claim illumination
Of soul and mind,
All the while
Mocked
By the dry, barren sands
Of life's forsaken shores,
Pitied
By devastating howling winds
That bear witness
To the futility
Of self-glorification.

Unlike shadows,

Realities wholly alive,
Embracing possibility,
Glimmer in His love –
It is for these that life shines
And Truth smiles
And all creation rejoices –
Even the atoms.
These,
With compassionate hearts,
And goodness their gift,
Extend love's warm embrace
To all –
Even those
Embodiments of dark shadows,
Who cause the earth to weep,
And the seas to groan,
And humankind to fail
And falter.

Fleeting shadows, have your fling!

Your triumph will not endure!
Soon will you fade away
To be no more,
Your final resting place,
The cold, forsaken ground
Of loss
And oblivion.

For the Sun has risen,
And hearts are ashine,
And glee blows upon the wind,
And Truth –
Great Slayer of shadows –
Will conquer, as it always has,
And always will,
Even forevermore.

13. Floating Speck of Dust

Floating speck of dust,

Released traveler
Speeding on your way,
How grand your sojourn
From where I stand.

In wonder,

I observe your wanderings
Through sunlit skies.
Do you traverse the moon
And defy its gravity,
Or does it just seem that way?
Have you seen the sun –
Up close, I mean?
And, if so,
Did you dance in its light
And bask in its rays?

Are you an angel with wings,

That you move so freely,
Untrammeled
By earthly cares and woes and wants?
Or are you a sign of resignation,
A guide to contemplate?

Your detachment is breathtaking.

You seem to resist the pull of earth itself,
Unwilling to descend to the ground below.
How I admire your aversion for all things lowly.

When His lovers pass by,

You move with an animation
That surpasses any known choreography.
Has their sacrifice moved you,
Or is it your love for them that stirs you?

Floating speck of dust,

Rejoicing orb in a translucent sky,
Would that I could emulate your obedience
To His will and law.
You have lessons to teach me.
Dance and I will learn.

Wing on!

Excite my imagination!
Exemplify what I might be,
Should I, too,
By His gentle winds and will,
Soar beyond the clouds.

14. From His Pen

From His Pen

God's Holy Breath is born –
Scripts and Scrolls
That soar as mighty waves
Upon celestial seas,
That surge as oceans of light
Cresting beyond the sands
And shores of eternity
Where only Holiness
Dares to sail
The awesome gales
Of Mystery.

From His Hand

Brilliant orbs of light
Are born.
They shine gloriously,
Transcending
Endless mystical skies
Of bejeweled truths
In the Sunlit immensity
Of the faithful soul.

Before the awesome majesty

Of God's Commanding Word,
Creation,
Now swooning away
Before undulating waves
Of Revelation,
Is breathless, dumbfounded.
Mysteriously restored,
She comes to life
With deep,
Life-giving breaths of joy.
Eager to imbibe
The Sweet Wine pouring forth,
She listens to Songs of Love
Played on the empyreal harp
Of Transcendence,
Each melody carried aloft
On vibrating luminosity.

From rhapsodic, whirling Scripts

Ordained
By the Center and Axis
Of worlds beyond time and measure,
Rapture and ecstasy
Embrace,
Dance swiftly atop the eternal skies
Of the spirit,
Inebriated
From the Winemaker's
Ruby Wine of Love
Poured from His emerald casks.
Of Ancient Wisdom.

From the inkwell of His Love

A myriad vineyards flourish
With fruits that make merry
The weary heart.
These bestow heavenly joy and rapture
From overflowing founts
Of faithfulness and constancy.

From His Pen

Revelation Sublime,
Preexistent,
Ordained by the Author
Of Creation's Eternal Scroll,
"Be" was born, stirred, moved
At His behest,
Then gave rise to love, knowledge,
Certitude and laughter.

From its swirling lines
Darkness is exposed, shamed, banished
To a cavernous deep to weep away
Its condign plight
Born of a haughty arrogance
Before its Lord.

From His Pen

God's Holy Breath is born –
Scripts and Scrolls
Ordained
To span the skies
And plummet the depths
Of every soul
Now,
And throughout
Eternity. –
We need but see
What He has written.

15. His Mercy

Waves,

Foreboding,
Relentless,
Raging Himalayan swells,
Heaving,
Surging,
In roaring crescendos
Of condign retribution –
Satanic storms from the depths of hell –
Rush relentlessly towards us.

Tumultuous billows,

Violent black mountains
Cresting deep in space,
Their depths fixed in the murky deep
Of the satanic self,
Speed upon the shores of our generation,
Jaws set wide
To devour land and life,
To swallow history and art,
All that was
And is,
To leave oblivion
Our only legacy.

Before the all-engulfing fury

We stand paralyzed,
Trembling,
Awestruck,
Firm in our collective
Unrepentance,
Yet unprepared to die,

Inexplicably,

Instantly,
Assuredly by the breaths of God,
Softly towering waves
Of light and grace
Unfold
From the monster sea
To bathe,
Soothe us
In warm dreams
And illumined hopes,
To bequeath endless tomorrows,
To loosen
The hardened grip
Of worldly desire
And set us free.

Renewed,

Confirmed,
We take up arms:
Faith and perseverance,
Arise to boldly challenge,
Struggle against,
Dark,
Engulfing forces,
Assured,
As we move towards
Our destiny,
Of His
Enduring love,
Timeless mercy.

16. I No Longer Hear Their Song

Musings on a fall morning

I no longer hear their song,

Those feathered angels of flight,
Or witness their flutter,
Intriguing,
To a watchful eye.
Is it to warmer climes
Of sun-drenched days,
And zephyrs fair
Caressing windflowers
Lavish with color
That they fly?

Their dancing I no longer see,

Their proud posture
And plump breasts,
Paraded for all to enjoy
As they perch upon a branch,
Are missed by eager eyes
And wondering hearts.

But seasons will pass

And spring will come
As surely
As the morrow's dawn,
And with it
Those flying marvels
That build their nests,
And raise their young,
And fly joyously
Amidst bush and tree,
All the while,
And unknowingly,
Praising their Maker,
And fulfilling,
With perfection,
Their destiny.

17. In Search of Purity

Fury,

Unrestrained,
Tearful
Before creation,
Permeating kindness
And rage,
Informing paradigm
And dimension,
Blazes
Through the inner reaches
Of the human soul,
In search of purity.

Brilliant bursts of hope

Radiate
From its impassioned quest.
They fade away,
Obscure,
And unrequited.

Bone and blood,

Like heart and mind,
Are captive
To its searching ferocity.
The clay of earthly force
Succumbs to its intensity,
The pure of heart
Relish it,
The dark of heart
Shake before its vehemence.

Noble maiden,

Purity,
Reveal thyself,
Lest humanity,
Captive to its play,
Turn to ash
In the gusting flames
Of separation
That, relentlessly,
Singe its soul.

Sweet purity,

Maid of heaven,
Return,
Unveiled,
Chaste,
And claim
Your rightful throne.
As do we,
Beauty requires you
And, alas,
She has fled from us, too!

18. In the Claw of the Eagle

In the Claw of the Eagle,

Held hard in His grasp –
Soft, gentle, truly tender –
Imprisoned In His Talons
High above earthly care,
The soiled madness
Of worldly schemes –
This I long for.

In the Claw of the Eagle,

Plucked from the mire
Of material pursuits –
Craggy wastelands
Of selfish desire –
Heart and mind relinquish
Fleeting fancies,
Dreams ill-formed.

In the Eye of the Eagle,

Creation humbled,
Surrenders
To Vision All-Embracing.
With this He finds
Heavenly souls,
Sanctified,
Eager to fly
In His clutch,

Above the
Deceiving carnival
Of frivolous pursuits,
Distracting din
Of hollow,
Echoing laughter,
The caged worship
Of vain,
Illegitimate imaginings.

In the Heart of the Eagle,

Power,
Transformative,
To raise those that crawl
The sidewalks of confusion
And consternation,
The dark alleys of despair
And degradation,
Into song birds,
Warblers of Truth,
Melodious,
High fliers circling,
Enraptured,
The verdant, fruit laden,
Tree of Life,
Doves in supernal skies
Of compassion, perception,
Triumph of self –
Low ground of abasement.

In the Claw of the Eagle –

Covenant Most Great –
Staunch, firm,
This,
My ardent wish.

In the Eye of the Eagle –

All-Encompassing –
Goodness may He find,
Pleasing May I be.

In the Heart of the Eagle –

Nest of Grandeur,
Holiness –
May I find acceptance,
Unworthy though my soul,
That I might shelter
Beneath the indomitable wings
Of His protection,
Held close
To the bosom
Of His Love.

19. In the Shadow of the Eagle

In the shadow of the eagle

Let me fly,
High and fast,
Upon sunlit, flowing zephyrs
Where mountain peaks kiss the winds
And caress endless sky;
Where clouds laugh and dreamers dream
Of lassoing the moon with words
Of poetic verse,
Every letter born of moonglow;
Where would-be angels
Wish that, they, too,
Might nest and soar on high,
Sky dancers choreographed
By the damsel of Nature
While she dances upon
Thrilling, rushing breezes
Of artful creativity.

In the shadow of the eagle,

Free, serene,
Rising high, diving low,
Gliding over, sliding down
Rainbows,
Dancing through hills
And above mountain streams,
Acrobat of the air –
Is this too much to wish for?

And yet,

In the shadow of the eagle,
Exhilarating though it be,
I am still bound,
Chained
To earth and cloud,
Wind and moon,
Nature's tavern
Of delights.

In the shadow of the eagle,

To soar high,
Mightily ascend
The spiritual heavens
Of His shining Love,
No soul can do,
Nor earthly wings
Reach so high.

For it is to the Sun of Truth

I long to fly,
Where angels nest
And heavenly beings reside;
Where lovers' songs
Are of another world
And soft flowing winds
Are born of spirit;
Where life is carved,
Ever so gently,
From love;
And the flight and stillness
Of souls
Is to the movement
Of the Baton of His Command;
Where the Orchestra of the Spirit
Plays sweet melodies
Of Supernal Love
That rise and fall
With harmonies celeste,
All born of His Holy Word.
It is to this realm
I long to fly!

In the Sunlight

Of the royal Falcon,
Winged Vicegerent
Of the One True God,
It is there I wish to nest,
Move at His Command,
Be illumined
By the Light of His Pleasure,
To be where angels soar,
And martyrs –
Heroes and heroines
Of Yazd, Tabarsi, Zanjan,
Nayriz and Tihran –
Circle in adoration,
Humbled
Before the Eternal, Risen Sun
Of God's
Most Holy Being.

It is there,

In that Presence,
That my heart,
Unworthy of note,
And my soul,
A harsh,
Barren wasteland,
In peals of undying hope,
Yearns to pay homage,
Flutter about
Forevermore
From branch to Branch,
In the Sunlit Skies
Of He Who proclaims:
"I am the royal Falcon
On the arm of the Almighty.
I unfold the drooping wings
Of every broken winged bird
And start it on its flight."[1]

[1]Bahá'u'lláh

20. Innocence

Innocence,

Elusive,
Wandering minstrel
Of a time gone by,
Have you no journeys
Through our climes?

Your melodious voice,

Soft, sweet,
So filled with promise,
Beckoning us to follow
In your footsteps
Is missed.
Deeply,
Grievously missed.

It has left a void

Where purity once dwelt.
Her longings for you
Proved unbearable –
Her tears engulfed her,
Carrying her far beyond our sight.
In the nighttime we hear her weeping.
At those times,
The moon refuses its light.

Innocence,

Begetter
Of a quiet beauty,
Soft voice
For the human heart,
Come and dwell amongst us.
Your songs will calm our souls.
These we will sing together.
Perhaps, then,
Purity,
Hearing our harmonies,
Will join us once more.

21. Lonely Branch

Lonely branch,

Stripped of all beauty
That was yours,
I see you barren
In the cold, hard days
Of winter,
Deprived of even
An appreciative glance
From passersby
And those who once rejoiced
In your splurge of green.

Lonely branch,

You seem so forlorn,
Incapable of, once again,
Smiling at the sun
Or gaily bathing,
Refreshed,
In springtime showers.

With a gentleness belying

Her seeming demise,
I heard her call –
"O, you, with a loving eye
And tender heart,
Do you not see
My destiny?
For the Lord has granted me
Sleep and rest
In the seeming cold
Of winter –
A time of rejuvenation
So that,
Once again,
From this lowly branch,
Verdure will spring forth,
Alive,
Energetic,
Reaching high for the sun,
Witnessing rainbows,
And catching raindrops
With the glee
Of a young child at play."

"And, then, O, friend,

I will gladden eye
And heart.
Such is the lesson
My Maker has beckoned me
To teach.
For from the icy winter,
Seemingly desolate,
Springs forth,
Once again,
The Springtime of His Love
To rejuvenate
All created things
And, yes,
Every human heart that will,
Like me,
Turn to Him."

22. Love Songs

Love songs,

Melodies from the heart,
Ring through my soul.
Song-laden winds
Intoned through forests
Of Divine Unity,
Dance through my reality.
Rapturous vibrations,
Unstoppable,
In paeans of joy,
Proclaim His Love.

Ethereal harmonies

Rise from the page
And soar amidst the angels –
Inimitable orchestrations
Vibrating to the shrill
Of His moving Pen –
Then resonate through universes
Beyond eternity
And the far vaster expanses
Of His Mighty Covenant.

Streaming notes of fidelity

Swirl through mystic skies
Painting every horizon
With compositions of Promise,
Fulfillment,
Oneness.

Nature,

Alive to charmed tunes
Softly sung
From countless excited atoms,
Yields to Love's
Newly written lyrics,
Then cries out,
As does His Pen,
The Call to Truth
And Inspiration
To those
Courageous enough
To hear,
Alive enough
To believe.

23. More than the Pen Can Hold

Albeit the heart swells more

Than the pen can hold,
Yet, I craft lines of praise,
And ply with coarse hand
The poet's craft.

I grasp for words

To stir the soul in love of Him.
So crudely I fail
To call Him to heart and mind
That the paper shrinks in shame
And the ink recoils,
Abashed,
Its words as naught.

I beg forgiveness

For my sin –
My errant pen,
Unfaithful to its trust,
Yields not a worthy word –
But what am I to do?
I have not gift of tongue or pen,
I have not wealth of thought
Or riches of mind.

I am but a lowly soul,

A seeming peasant
On the spiritual path
With but one desire,
To be bereft of all but Him.

So take my heart

And take my soul.
Take my life and free my blood,
And let it pour down like copious rain
From clouds
Of His Command.

Then,

Yes, perhaps, then,
My heart will soar
And my pen will fly,
And my soul,
Empowered with the crimson ink
Of love,
Will pen
On the plane of sacrifice,
Flowing red words of love
Mingled with the martyr's dance,
Words that sear the heart
With racing flames
Undeniable,
For all to see.

And if it be His Will –

And for this I pray,
May those fallen,
Crimson words of love,
Scattered and embraced
By earthly ground,
Combine to touch some heart,
And thus,
Should it be His Pleasure,
Be acceptable to even
Him.

24. Mystic Dancer

In honor of those whose lives, on the pathway of Truth, were taken from them.

Mystic dancer,

Relentless blue flames
Dance at your core.
Choreographed in love,
Faith and fidelity proceed from you
As you dance upon earthly atoms
Of a celestial path,
Your being wreathed in joy,
Your soul writhing in pain
For the endemic blindness
Of cold, steel hearts.
Onlookers are abashed,
Struck dumb
By your winsome grace
And form.

Flames of love

Ignite
Within the chambers of your heart
And burst forth
Through breast and bone
To impassion and illumine
Your being.
Now you move in Godly two-step
To the brutal,
Penetrating crack of the whip
In the martyr's chorus.
Unrestrained as interstellar lights,
You dance without shadow,
Your feet without skin.

Mystic dancer,

Leap! Leap!
Leap once more
Over hate and rancor!
Approach
The Beloved's door!
Cry His Name!
Bear no ill
Though stones are hurled.
You walk the long corridor
Of love's trials,
Leaving darkness far behind
And rapture near.

Mystic lover

Of mystic blood,
Relentless blue flames
Dance at your core
Choreographed in endurance,
Staunchness and proof.
But, alas,
Of sweet, red blood
You have none.
From flowing rivers
To trickling streams
To last drop,
It fueled
Your mystic flame
For His
Mystic Love
In the mystic journey
From God unto God.

25. Not Mist, or Rain, or Stormy Day

Poetry,

Not mist,
Or rain,
Or Stormy day,
Can keep you from me –
I seek you
As the jolted lover,
Writhing in anguish,
Seeks solace
For his shattered,
Trampled heart.

I hear you

In the thunder
Of blazing white lightning
And roar
Of billowing,
Belching volcanos.
I hear your rhyme
On zephyrs intoning melodies
Only violins play,
In gentle breezes
Of orchestral harmonies
Caressing
Flower and bloom
In gardens remote
And near
Where doves coo,
And warblers sing,
Where lovers dance,
And spirits chant
God's praises.

No rustling leaf

Is without you,
No grain of sand
Or mighty stone
That does not
Proclaim
Your timeless
Longevity,
The broad sweep
Of your riveting power,
Your unmistakable,
Inimitable,
Voicings.

Poetry,

You can not
Hide from me,
Nor evade
My passionate,
Relentless pursuit!
Your visage –
Too fair,
Too beauteous,
Your cheeks
Too blushed
To be taken for another –
Shines
As the Pleiades.
In the hallowed precincts
Of your bosom,
Mystic brilliance
From your luminous deep
Abashes the moon,
Its light retreating
Deep into the caverns
Of its scarred visage.

Poetry,

Walk with me!
I yearn
To hold you tight,
Press you close,
Dance your words
And lines
On stages
Where gaiety and joy,
Profundity and meaning,
Play to ears
Softened
To the stories you tell,
The truths,
Old and new –
For they are one –
You romance
When the poet's tryst
Invokes
Your magic.

Poetry,

Sweep me away!
My heart,
Eager to fly
Where angels soar
And souls take wing
As birds of flight,
Awaits your call.

Reach out,

Sweet verse!
Hold me close!
Then let us traverse
The beckoning skies
Of Transcendence,
Ride upon
Nature's bounteous clouds
Of Eternal Love,
And ride
The fast-rushing gales
Of all that is,
Hand in hand,
Together,
Rapturous,
As one.

26. Pass the Wineskin

Intoxicated lovers,

Inebriated with the Wine of Love,
Tell us your tale
And pass the wineskin.
Let us drink deeply, too,
Of your Ruby Wine.

What is it that you imbibe

That pours like fire and shines like light?
From what cask did it come?
What name the Winemaker?
What street the tavern?

Intoxicated lovers,

Take to the streets and dance.
The world has never seen your like.
It stumbles to describe your
Perfect sobriety.
It pales before your paradox.

Then walk in sober, straight lines

For all to see.
The mystic path is more manifest
Than the heavens,
Calling more loudly than rushing gales.

Intoxicated lovers,

Inebriated with the Wine of Love,
Let us, too, revel in the sweetness
That sets veins on fire
And stirs every limb,
That inebriates the soul
And clears the mind.

Pass the wineskin,

Lest I seize it from your hands!
Pass the Ruby Wine of Heaven.
The Beloved awaits
The inebriated of heart
And mine is still unmoved.
Pass the wineskin!
An intoxicated lover
I, too,
Yearn to be!

27. Petals Fall

In honor of those whose lives, on the pathway of Truth, were taken from them.

I saw them fall,

One by one,
Petals
Of the Rose Garden
Of His Love.

In hues

Of crimson red,
Testimony to sacrifice,
And fragrance pure
And holy –
Truly attar of soul –
Sanctified
Above worldly pursuits
And the cleric's wrath,
They fall,
One by one,
Lovers of His Beauty,
Recipients of,
And condemned by,
The ugly,
Dark mask
Of tyranny,
Worn
By the living dead
Who dwell
In the sepulchers
Of the demonic self,
Comfortably reposed,
Unknowingly,
In tombs
Of Evil –
Satan
Their only fast,
Bosom
Companion.

I saw them fall,

Soul by soul,
Petals
In the Sanctuary
Of the Beloved,
Illumined,
Velvety soft,
Glistening
In their triumph,
Radiant
In their love,
Magnificent
In their rise
To Paradise.

28. Resplendent Rainbows

Resplendent rainbows,

Illumined arcs
Betokening God's Covenant,
Heaven-splashed colors
Ruling supreme in a brilliant sky,
What message have you to tell?

Is it that your beaming red

Proclaims boldly
The spilt blood of God's lovers,
Martyrs to His Revelation,
The propelling Force
To unify all peoples?

Or is it that your green signifies

The verdure of springtime?
Or, perhaps,
The deep, luminous emerald green
Of a soul illumined,
Growing spiritually
In His love,
Unveiled as a lavish,
Green landscape
Of spirituality –
Yet all the while afire
With Him
Who is the Source
Of all Fire –
He Who gives Light
And Love
To universes seen
And unseen?

Gazing on your

Sunlit yellow,
My heart cries out
To the All-Glorious Beloved –
O, Sun of Truth!
O, Brilliant Orb
In a darkened universe!
Bathe my soul
In Your Most Great
Light!
O, Source of Life!
Warm my being
With Your Holy Word,
Inspiration,
And Love.

Resplendent rainbows,

Your many colors
I ponder –
Such unity in diversity
Cannot be easily dismissed.
Your call is high and reigns
Over hill and vale.
Is it that we are one?
That our destiny –
Peoples of all colors –
Is to rise high
And shine brightly,
As the colors you so boldly
Proclaim?

Whatever your tale,

I know not.
But my heart
Sings your praises
Knowing this –
Upon your beauty
And paints of light
I reflect –
Then ponder
Truth and purpose,
Lights within that,
Like a rainbow,
Shine resplendent
In the many hues
Of life's meaning –
These against the blue skies
Of my joyously awakened soul.

29. Rippling Coquettes

Rippling coquettes
On the pond of dreams,
Gently stream
To water's edge,
Where reverie and hope
Glisten as one,
And aspirations nourish
The pensive imagination.

Ripples,

Flirtatious to my very soul,
Course to the shore
Where dreams and reality
Stare and tarry
Until they move on
To sunlit enclaves
Where lovers tryst.

Rippling coquettes,

Proffer but one
Dream
That I may grasp
And hold.
I have been away too long
And there is little in my heart
For my feet to dance to.

Ripples,

Timeless, endless,
One with the wistful breeze,
Water my waiting soul
Like waves pounding
Water-patient sands.

Bear me no restraint.

Fill the vessel of my longing
With dreams that only
Dreamers dream.
Till then,
I can dream
No more.

30. Shadows of Truth

Shadows of Truth,

Black upon the stone walls
Of a hardened heart,
Alive with color to the awakened soul
Vibrating to the Call of the Beloved –
Sway to rapturous melodies
And harmonies of a Place –
A Condition –
Beyond illusion, self and passion,
And pursuits that hug –
Nay, cling to! –
The mire
And swamplands
Of doubt and disbelief.

Shadows,

Whisper-soft,
Seemingly silent,
Thunderingly eloquent,
Tell their tale
In palettes of soaring
Light
Upon the hearts and souls,
And awakened minds
Of His lovers
Of all that might be,
And all that is to come,
When the soul takes its flight
To the luminous, celestial Garden
Of the Great Reality,
The true abode
Of all who seek it.

31. Silence Lost

Silence Lost

To deafening confusion,
Where have gone
Your retreats of reflection
And quietude?
Seduced
By the din of inconsequence,
Might they have plunged
Into the thoughtless core
Of meaning lost?
Or, perhaps they collapsed
Into the crushing gravitation
Of illusion,
Fancy,
And self.
I think I hear their lamentation
From the graveyard
Of the forgotten.

Silence lost

To bursts and thrusts
Of superficiality,
What haven remains
That I might find you there?
For my soul is withering
And my heart forlorn.

From deep within my soul

Rises the quiet crescendo of reply –
"From within, not without
O, lover of the Beloved,
And seeker after His Beauty,
Restful havens of reflection
And redolent gardens of quietude
Replete with meaning can be found.
Through them flow the streaming
Waters of His Revelation
And the murmuring brooks
Of His Remembrance
And praise.
Reside therein –
Blissful peace,
Abiding joy,
And sweet silence –
These, eagerly
Await you."

32. Songbird

Songbird,

Born of forests
Lavish in splashes luxuriant,
Lush green,
Awash in colors and hues
Angels envy, ponder –
It seems your beauteous,
Captivating trills
Descend
From some Godlike paradise,
Orchestral to its core,
Where notes pure,
Songs primordial,
Yet new, refreshed,
Come forth,
Then dance upon the winds,
To thrill, enchant,
Release joy
In receptive hearts.

Songbird,

How blessed you are!
Your melodies,
Softly sung,
Quietly whispered
Truths
Carried treetop to treetop
To be unfolded,
Performed,
In heavenly tones
And voice –
These,
Sunbeams alone –
And the glow of moon
And stars –
Dare testify
To the stories –
And glories –
They bear,
Tell.
Pure light,
Alone,
Sings
Your mysteries!

Songbird,

Delicately held in Nature's hand,
How reminiscent of ancient love,
The tryst of hearts,
Love's timeless embrace,
Your sweet songs!
And what melodies are these
That you sing?
Is it
The Nightingale of Paradise
That you seek?
His Melodious Call
That you eagerly await,
Long for,
Yearn to hear,
That it fill your being
With bliss,
Rest,
Repose?

Songbird,

Like you,
I search,
Cry out for,
Impatiently await,
The Enchanting Melodies
And Rapturous Song
Of the Beloved,
He Who pens
Ethereal Notes into Sublime Song,
Who,
Within the Paradise
Of His Being,
Strums
Celestial Strings
And Chords
On the storied harp
Of eternal realities.

Songbird

Nestled in earthly trees!
The bird of my heart,
Impatient,
Restless
On the branch of longing,
Yet hopeful,
Eagerly listens
For the alluring,
Mighty Call
Of God's Promised Royal Falcon,
Whose Melodies,
In this Day,
Intone all Truth.
Perhaps, I hear it now:
"O bird of every longing heart!
Fear not!
Do not despair!
My outspread wings welcome you!
My ancient beating heart,
Timepiece of all creation,
And the rushing,
Pulsating rivers of My Love
Are here to revive you!
Speed forth, then, O weary bird,
On the wings of the spirit!
Perch upon the sanctified,
Faithful Branch!
Find rest, repose,
Sheltered

Beneath the Canopy
Of My Love
Amidst the Divine Forests
Of Revelation!

For the Beauteous,

Bell-like Tones
Of the Beloved,
Ringing throughout creation
And beyond its mighty ramparts,
Call you!
Embrace their Resounding Melodies,
For these, alone,
Quiet,
Gladden,
Give peace,
To the restive souls
And longing hearts,
Of Truth's
Adoring lovers.

33. Sounds Lost

Nightingales of love,

Where have you flown?
I miss your sweet,
Soul-searching warblings
In rose gardens
Where pure lovers tryst,
Redolent remembrances
Embrace,
Holy romance
Searches endlessly,
High and low,
For the
Matchless Beauty,
Be it but a glimpse,
A move of the hand.

Breezes of understanding

Whistling
Through the leaves
And branches of time,
I no longer hear
The wisdom you once carried
Softly
Through the astonishment-lined
Avenues of my soul.
Have our lives,
Dull to wonder and contemplation,
Driven you far
From the still pond
Of the heart,
Thunderous awakenings
Of mind?

Love songs,

Tender, timeless,
Where do your melodies
Now play?
Your lyrics of felicity,
Rapture,
Affection,
No longer grace
The page.
Have they gone the way
Of love's harmonies
Lost?
It seems so,
For the din
Of displeasure and divide,
Only,
Are left
To echo endlessly
In the cold, dark rooms
Of frivolity
And unhappiness.

My heart,

Quiet and still,
Reflective,
Now responds with hope,
Assurance –
"All these things
Will surely pass,
For He,
The Bringer of Joy,
Transcendence,
Fulfillment,
Has come.
And soon,
An awakened humanity
Will hear
The nightingales of love
And wonder,
The sweet-scented winds
Of rapturous understanding,
God-given
Melodies and harmonies
Of the heart."

To these Glad Tidings,

The mention of His Names,
All atoms of creation –
Enthralled,
Vibrating orchestral strings
Of Truth
Bowed by God's Will –
Testify,
Rejoice
To the celestial,
Resounding peals
Of the New Day.
We have,
Simply,
To listen.

34. Stars in the Heaven of Understanding

In honor of those whose lives, on the pathway of Truth, were taken from them.

I saw them climb

Beyond the clouds,
Ascending to the heavens
Where brilliant stars dwell,
Their beauteous forms
Deftly moving step by step
On the stairway to their Beloved,
Their luminous souls serene
As they danced on the zephyrs
That only lovers touch.

Their ascent complete,

They took their place
In star-filled skies,
Shining boldly
For those with eye
And heart
To see.

Their quiet, scarred shells

Remain with us,
A testimonial to Faith,
Desecrated by infamy,
An indictment on humanity.
But the luminous pearls
Of their being
Ascended to supernal
Realms of faithfulness
To dwell in His Presence,
Circle round His Court.

The Call of the New Day

Bade them arise.
Their response was
Blood-red, glorious;
Ours,
A grasping quiet
Of words unspoken,
Effete to describe
The impassioned calm
Of last countenance.

Stars in the heaven of understanding

The Beloved has called them.
So shall we.

35. The Babble of the Dead

O friend!

Be not troubled
By the babble of the dead,
They whose words, loathsome,
Like dying breaths of a devoured dragon,
Repel
Seekers of Truth,
Those on the Path of True Knowledge.

These, lovers of the All-Beauteous –

Omniscient Axis
Of His all-pervading creation –
Soar high above the charred, lifeless ground
Of misguided love, selfish, self-serving
Worldly pursuits.
Words of artful sophistry, masked,
Deceive them not.

O friend in Truth!

The babble of the living dead
Fall to the ground in infamous humiliation,
Lay as trampled, crumbled bone,
Then turn to dust, forsaken,
Gripped in ridicule by mocking winds
And contemptuous gales –
The mire of the self-absorbed,
Their final resting place.

O friend on the Path of Love!

Let us fly to sweeter climes,
Where spirits laugh and play
And gaiety abounds,
Where the cherubim,
On lyre and lute,
Make merry,
Play luminous melodies,
Sing translucent, celestial song.

There,

Transforming, life-renewing Words,
All-powerful, ever-merciful –
Heavenly Behests of the Beloved –
Adorn Book and Tablet,
Raise creation on pillars lifted high
By the Unseen, Lord of Might.

From each letter

Gushing rivers of Love flow;
Mountains of Wonderment
Proudly stand and tower;
Seas of Ancient Wisdom
And Oceans of Understanding
Move to energizing rhythms
Below kindred, sweeping winds
Of purpose, faith, certitude.

O intoxicated nightingale

In the Rose Garden of His Love!
Let us dance through every page,
Rejoice to the honeysuckle scent of every line,
Wing heart and soul through the illumined Paradise
Of His Revelation.

Then,

Should it please Him,
Let us immerse in the surging Waters
Of His love;
Ride the silver, luminous crests
Of longing desire;
Surf the onrushing waves of Truth
And Oneness;
Swim the crystal waters
Of His praise.

For Truth,

Sweet, Holy Truth,
Does the true seeker yearn!

For Oneness,

Humanity's saviour,
Does the true lover rejoice!

For love of the All Glorious Beloved –

And love of no other –
Does the impassioned lover, lost in rapture,
Wandering in the vale of ecstasy,
And embraced by the welcoming arms
Of the Beloved,
Eagerly, gladly,
Give praise,
Live
And die!

36. The Birds Sing and Dance

The birds sing and dance,

As willed by Him,
That we may hear
His Song.
The grass moves in the breeze,
At His pleasure,
That we may recount the Movement
Of His Pen.
The leaves soar aloft
In a seemingly magical choreography,
In obedience to His Command,
That we may rejoice
In His uplifting Name
And exalted Revelation.

The stars shine in abashment

Before His Radiance –
And this, too, He has willed.
The moon, humbled
By His Splendrous Beauty,
Rises only
To please Him.

The human heart –

O, the human heart! –
Unique mirror that it is,
Divinely crafted to reflect
The brilliance of His Shining –
This,
And this, alone,
In willful blindness
And self-adoration,
Dares question
The magnificence of the Divine Sun
And its blazing Eternal Glory –
The sole Source
Of its joy
And happiness.

37. The Human Heart

Land of Prophets

And ancient rhyme,
Where love
And lovers
Tryst,
And pain
And joy embrace,

Fertile ground

In which wisdom
Springs
To spring eternally,
In which culture
Grows
And reaches harvest,

A land so rich

It is womb to the arts
And beauty fair,
Where tapestries are woven
From pure threads
Of ethos
And pathos
Into the stories
Of our years.

This land,

Closer than life
Or hopelessly far,
Of great, wide horizons
And dawning points
Of peace,
Etched
With streams of wonderment
And waters limpid,

Where strangers abide

Or do not,
Where life is lived
And lives on,
Such is the beauteous,
Beloved land
We call the human heart.

38. The Inner Reality

The inner reality

Is a world of light and shadows,
Of paradox,
Not contradiction,
Where veiled free will
And a surging collective destiny
Meet, flow, merge
Into a new creation.

In its realm lights are cast,

Probing timeless
Questions of existence,
So that truth is sought,
Embraced,
Setting its myriad lovers free
To be enslaved
To its beauty.

In its blackest hours

It is a night
Of darkened streets
On which no lights shine,
Only feeble, human –
Or subhuman – globes.
These, like flickering fluorescents,
Cast an unnatural light
On a lurid existence.

Like the child,

The inner reality
Delights in instructive play.
Challenge is the playground
On which it must exert,
Fall, fail, excel.
Structured, informed lessons follow –
Test it, forge it,
Awaken it to possibilities
Unimagined, unharnessed.

Nobility is its origin

And destiny,
The endless spring
Of an eternal youth,
Gushing, culminating,
Rising mountain-high
In founts of mind and heart

Only to be released,

Empowered,
Harnessed,
In the charging falls
Of a relentless quest
For meaning,
Purpose,
Truth.

Infinite, folded possibilities

Reside within its core,
Beckon us,
Remain restless within us,
Until we call them forth
To be released,
Evolve,
Exert themselves –
Transform us.

The inner reality

Where humankind is tested,
And character is forged,
Where light and shadow meet
And luminosity must ultimately triumph,
Relentlessly beckons.
Ours is to listen,
To hear,
To be the call.

39. The Soul Within

Brilliant beams,

Spun from threads of light,
Emerge
From a crystalline heart
Deep within the lover's bosom –
They race
In wrapped radiance
And shine brightly
From portals of love –
The luminous eyes
Of the enthralled lover,
Afire
With the Beloved's
Countenance.

Each sparkling beam,

Each luminous thread,
Is born of love,
Joy,
The sacred,
These tenderly nurtured,
Encouraged,
In limpid chambers
Of gemlike,
Living beauty.

In contrast,

Emptiness and loneliness –
Unmasked woe
Embedded deep within –
Take form
In the unlit hollows
And stretching, narrow halls
Of a meandering,
Passive existence.
They find their way
Through tunnels of dull, dark,
Unraveling hopes
To sullen,
Lifeless eyes. –
These know, too well,
The pitch-like night
Of unfulfilled dreams
And tears of sorrow
That weep their way
To the bleak,
Dank terrain
Of empty streets
Of barren loves,
Hopes fallen,
Joy lost.

Our eyes,

Our countenance,
Tell their tale,
Free of deceit or dissimulation.
They cannot hide
The truth they speak –
Happy or sad –
Of the soul
Within.

40. This Is Love

To lift a soul, weary, tired,

And raise him high,
This is love.

To carry a load, onerous, heavy,

Of another,
This is love.

To smile in the face of frowns

And doubting eyes,
This is love.

To extend a hand to souls in disbelief

That another could care,
This is love.

To speak with words soft as fallen snow

When reviled by an angry heart,
This is love.

To see beauty in every soul

Despite indwelling darkness,
This is love.

To give hope and care, wish others well

Though no kindness be returned,
This is love.

To do all these,

So simple yet hard of accomplishment,
This is love.

To humble ourselves

Should we do some good,
Knowing all love pours down
From Clouds of Grace
On raindrops from the All-Merciful,
This, my friend,
Is love.

41. Thunderous falls

Thunderous falls

Galactic in dimension
Descend from heaven:
Onrushing torrents
Of light
And challenge;
Revolutionizing,
Vertical,
Swiftly moving seas
Of Revelation.

These inspire awe,

Humility,
Wonder;
Surround,
Flood,
Purify the planet
From ages-deep sediment;
Redefine
Every stream's bed
And ocean floor;
Cleanse
All ground from dross;
Render every soil
Fertile.

Pearls stir,

Rejoice,
Freed at last
From sand and shell,
Gleam
Amidst heaving
Waves of Grace,
Celestial surging walls
Of Benevolence
And Justice.

In godly quietude

The Beloved of All Universes
Watches,
Pleased
With all He sees.

With tender hands

And gentle touch,
Each pearl He picks,
Transforming luster
Into heavenly shining.

With these –

Brilliant spiritual realities,
Breathtaking, beauteous –
The Beloved,
With infinite love
And heavenly grace,
Adorns
The luminous sapphire skies
And ethereal realms
Of Paradise –
And this,
To all eternity.

42. Truth, Elude Me Not

Truth,

Elude me not –
Your beauteous countenance
Are my eyes'
Only destination.

Truth,

Hide not your charms –
A maid so fair
Should not dwell
Behind veils –
Even though those
Shades of darkness
Be my own.

Truth,

I hear your whispers
Blowing through the hollows
Of my soul –
But it is your voice,
Loud,
Resonant,
That I await.

Truth,

Gentle maiden
Bearing God's Knowledge,
Let me gaze
On your Mystic Pearls
And Gems of Holiness,
For, at last,
My heart,
Newly alive,
Welcomes you.
Come!
Reside therein!

43. Truth

It knows no boundaries

Or avenues it can not walk.
Light mimics its speed
And omnipresence.

It permeates creation and eternity

As waters fill the seas.
It surges within form and matter
And resonates endlessly
In their embrace.

All knowledge is its offspring,

All understanding
Mere glimpses
Of its beauty.
It heals all hurt and woe.

It lifts every bird

And speeds quantum harmonies
To the depths of every atom.
It begets galaxies and gravity
And solar winds.

It surrounds all,

Permeates all.
It is both alpha and omega.
It is the source of every wave,
The genesis of every drop.

Only the human heart

Can resist its force,
Only the human eye
Be blind to it.
No wonder the Beloved loves
The impassioned lovers
Who seek its casks
And drink its wine.
These, intoxicated,
Dwell in sober
Objectivity.

44. Upon the Bough

I saw a bird upon the bough,

And heard it whisper to the winds
Songs of love and longing,
Each so beauteous
As to be strummed by rainbows
And cooed by heavenly doves
Proudly perched upon lofty peaks
That only eagles claim.

I saw the wind

With tenderness godlike
Proffer,
With humility and grace,
Each song to soft and gentle
Awaiting clouds –
These, with reverence,
Clutched each note, each sound,
To their bosom,
Then offered them,
As if godly treasure
And with tears falling,
One by one,
To the highest heavens
Only angels know.

As if awakening from a dream,

I saw that all I beheld
Was within me,
Calling to be explored
Within deep recesses
Of my soul
Where winds of hope
Flow and dance
Upon the promise
Of sunlit, verdant,
Redolent tomorrows.

Within the bosom of my soul,

Seemingly bare and barren
But alive
With enchanting melodies
Of search,
Love and desperate yearning,
I heard a Voice
Speaking in tones of Light,
Beckoning me
To Him,
That He might
Take the coarse clay
Of my life
And transform it
Into a receptacle
Bearing the Holy Water
Of His Love,
Mystical Songs
And Ethereal Melodies
To would-be lovers
Who,
Like me,
Saw a bird upon the bough,
And heard it whisper to the winds
Songs of love and longing,
Each so beauteous
As to be strummed by rainbows
And cooed by heavenly doves
Proudly perched upon lofty peaks
That only eagles claim.

45. Upon the Winds

Upon the winds

Mystical voicings of ancient praise,
Intoxicating, stirring,
Voiced by a simple drop,
Seemingly ordinary,
Obscure,
Caught my ear,
Intrigued my soul.
Listening intently,
I heard rapturous melodies
Softly sung
In tones of unequivocal,
Abiding humility.
These, unabashedly,
Praised its Master,
The Great and Mighty Sea,
True Beloved
Of every knowing,
Faithful drop.

Wind and gale,

Zephyr and breeze,
So loved its whisperings
They filled air and sky
And heavens beyond
With resonant bell-like tones
That stirred
Within the realities
Of all things,
Even atoms
And searching hearts.

From this drop

Rushed forth a rising tide
Of spiritual understanding,
Cresting waves
Of soulful wisdom.
Its voice,
Pure, submissive,
Caused clouds to weep
At the sweetness
Of its praise,
Depths
Of its profundity.

Within the realities of all

Who dared to listen –
No less my soul –
This captivating praise
Penned lines
Of reflection and wonder
From the inkwell of astonishment,
Inscribed verses so sweet
That honeybees
Thought them flower,
Hummingbirds,
Crazed
By their sweetness,
Dwelt long,
Drank deep the succulent nectar
From their newly found,
Delectable,
Honeysuckle.

Its sweet,

Lofty themes,
Luminous, transcendent,
Transfixed my being –
Soaring words of praise and love
Cause hearts to swell,
Then pound
In unapologetic rhythm,
Mimicking
The beating drums
And eternal flows
Of Nature.
My soul,
Thrilled and unconstrained,
Celebrated
This strangely mystical Orchestration.

Wind,

Now too,
In all its forms,
Reposed in stillness,
It, too, transfixed,
By the anthems of praise
It unknowingly carried.
Joy and wonderment,
Breaths of life,
Filled its quieted lungs.

Each word

Of this humble drop
Engendered
Meaning,
Love unimagined.
These reverberated,
Chamber to chamber,
In hearts questing
For the Unknowable,
Eternal Beloved.

From this drop,

Greatness,
Like petals of a rose,
Unfolded before me.
Self-effacement
Strode boldly forward,
And humility,
Impatient,
Threw back its veil.
Darkness turned to light,
And blindness,
Beckoning Light,
Surrendered
To sight.

With time,

The wind began to blow,
Listening creatures
In multitudes
Went about their way
As before.
Had they heard, comprehended,
The lessons taught?
For pristine praise
And Truth,
Intoned in mystic tones
Of alluring beauty
Permeate all realities,
Free from bondage
The once-shackled,
Disconsolate soul.

From an obscure drop,

Swept away,
Exuberant,
In love of its Creator,
Anthems of Truth,
Arose,
Shone forth.
From seeming insignificance,
Soulful peals
Echoing
Throughout creation
Praised
The Great and Mighty Sea.

As to those who hear

And heed
The gentle whisperings
Of Truth
Riding,
Dancing upon,
The winds of the heart
And zephyrs of the soul –
Happiness unalloyed,
Joy without bounds,
Their allotted share!

46. What Wine Is This?

What wine is this

That fills ocean floors
And crescendos of scarlet waves?
That rains down lucid ruby drops
From heaven's crimson clouds?

What wine is this

That flows through space
And inebriates time?
That pours freely,
Though rarely,
In the casks of our lives?

What wine is this

That thrills my soul
As a raging river
Thrills its bed and shores?
That gives life to all who drink?

What wine is this

That eludes containment,
Yet is grasped in full
By the human heart?

What wine is this

Poured from the hand of the Beloved
For all who seek
The intoxication of His Presence?

The Wine of Life, my friend!

Drink deeply and revive!

47. What Words and Letters Are These?

What words and letters

Are these,
That splash across the page
And move in waves
Of Ethereal Beauty,
Powered
By the onrushing tide
Of Revelation?

What words and letters

Are these,
That masquerade in black
Then rise from the page
To soar
Amidst eternal,
Supernal Skies
Of Truth,
Then dive into vast,
Unimagined dimensions
Of Profundity,
Only to rise once more
From panting hearts,
And lips
Of lovers?

Such

Is the Word of God,
Creative,
Mysterious,
Unshackled
From time and place,
Born
Of the Pen of Glory –
Held dear,
And fast,
By adoring souls.

48. Whispers Upon the

Wind

What manner of love

Is this?
What secret
Do they share,
That they move as
Whispers
Upon the wind,
Then swirl across the page
In cursive, bold thought,
Their quest
Meaning,
Beauty,
And truth,
Embraced
In a choreography
Known only
To the unwritten –
Or half-written –
Page?

Relentlessly,

They strive to tell some tale,
Knowing not their end.
The ravages of time,
That test of worth

And beauty,
Alone,
Will seal their fate.

Then,

If these words be read,
And deemed not poor,
Peace
Will kiss the page,
And hands will raise it
Once again,
That whispers upon the wind
May be heard
By ear and heart,
And passed
From hand to hand,
To die but slowly,
Having lived
A page
Whose home
Is the heart,
And whose words
Have not been inscribed
In vain.

49. White Dove

Inspired by a white dove that flew across my path years ago in Michigan.

White dove,

Beauteous,
Ever gentle,
Ascendant grace
Amidst sunbeam skies
Of tranquility,
Freedom –
The Almighty's gift
To you –
Symbol
Of peace,
Humanity's transcendent
Destiny.

White dove,

Coo again
Nectar-sweet,
Softly flowing
Songs of love –
Testimony
To heavenly realms,
Harbinger
Of a oneness that must be –
They speak
Of the perfumed savors
Born
Of His Remembrance.
For we, too,
Long to soar in heavens
High above
The desert-dry sands
Of a parched, illusory,
Existence.

In your eyes

Truth
I see –
Undefiled
By the poisoning winds
Of unholy discourse –
And vision
To behold what is –
All that is –
With undimmed brightness,
Hope,
Clarity.

White dove,

Beauteous emissary
Of peace,
Living portrait
Of tranquility,
Snow-white purity
Born of Eternal Grace –
Fly high,
Unabashed,
Luminous in midday light
That awakened eyes
Might see
The story you tell.

For, in you,

Dove of supreme beauty,
I see humanity,
Unresigned to walk,
Seemingly dazed,
The dark,
Pitted, low ground
Of a mortal life,
But destined to soar,
Winged in Love
And Spirit,
Through vast skies
Of endless tomorrows
High aloft the mighty zephyrs
Of Destiny,
To dwell,
At last,
In the Celestial Realms
Of The Most Great Peace –
Promised Haven,
Sanctuary,
For all mankind.

50. Winds of Time

Winds of time,

Moving swiftly past
The threshold of my life,
What good might you find
On your endless, sacred scrolls,
Acceptable in His sight?
Was there some small right,
The absence of some great wrong,
That He might find worthy
When I ascend to the Great Beyond?
Did refinement elude me,
Or did I reach long, grasp hard
And hold it dear?

Winds of time,

Moving swiftly past
The threshold of my life,
Was there a breath I breathed,
Or step I walked,
A song I sang or rhyme I wrote,
That He will find pleasing
When the last nighttime falls?
In the theater of life,
Did my limbs quiver as I lived my lines?
Did I stand on the stage too long?
Or did I complete the act with alacrity,
Passion and resolve?

Winds of time,

Moving swiftly past
The threshold of my life,
I hear your howl and feel your force.
But it is your endless, sacred scrolls
I yearn for.
Its characters I long to ponder
That I might see my life
Through His eyes.

Winds of time,

Moving swiftly past
The threshold of my life,
Visions past I do not see.
Words of Truth you waft instead
From the Beloved of all hearts:
"Bring thyself to account each day . . ." [1]
This Wisdom penetrates my soul,
Purifies my reflections.
Your scrolls remain
For other days,
When His winds,
Alone,
Will lift me up
To see my life.

[1] Bahá'u'lláh: Hidden Words, Arabic Number 31

www.ingramcontent.com/pod-product-compliance
Lightning Source LLC
Chambersburg PA
CBHW021950120726
47992CB00001B/235